GUITAR TANGOS

BY WILLIAM BAY

WBM10
ISBN 978-0-9859227-7-1

© 2012 BY WILLIAM BAY
ALL RIGHTS RESERVED. INTERNATIONAL COPYRIGHT SECURED. B.M.I.

Visit us on the Web at www.williambaymusic.com

PREFACE

The tango is the king of the Latin dances. The captivating rhythms and seductive melodies of the tango have captured the imaginations of musicians and composers for many years. The tango has even found its place in the world of concert musical literature due to the fine works of composers such as Astor Piazzolla. It is hard to imagine a guitarist today without a number of tangos in his solo repertoire. These 14 tangos were composed to provide tango literature for the plectrum or flatpick guitarist. Of course they may also be performed on the classic guitar. I would like to make special note of the tango, *Lucia.* I originally wrote *Lucia* as a guitar duet. The duet is recorded on my *Acoustic Guitar Portraits* recording and is also in print in the companion book. I composed a new solo setting for *Lucia* in this book. I believe these tangos may be performed in concert or recital, for fun or even on a "gig". I hope you enjoy performing them as much as I did composing them!

It has been my desire to see the plectrum guitar utilized as a concert instrument in a manner similar to that of the classical guitar. My hope is that these studies may contribute to that goal. Other collections in this plectrum guitar series include **Short Etudes**, **Velocity Studies** *and* **Technic Etudes.** Additional plectrum guitar collections may be found on my website **www.williambaymusic.com**.

Recordings are available for some of the books in the William Bay music catalog. These recordings may be found at ***www.williambaymusic.com***. Please check my website for availability.

CONTENTS

Tango	Page
Tango 1	4
Tango 2	7
Tango 3	10
Tango 4	13
Tango 5	16
Tango 6	19
Tango 7	22
Tango 8	25
Tango 9	28
Tango 10	31
Tango 11	34
Tango 12	37
Tango 13	40
Lucia (Solo)	43

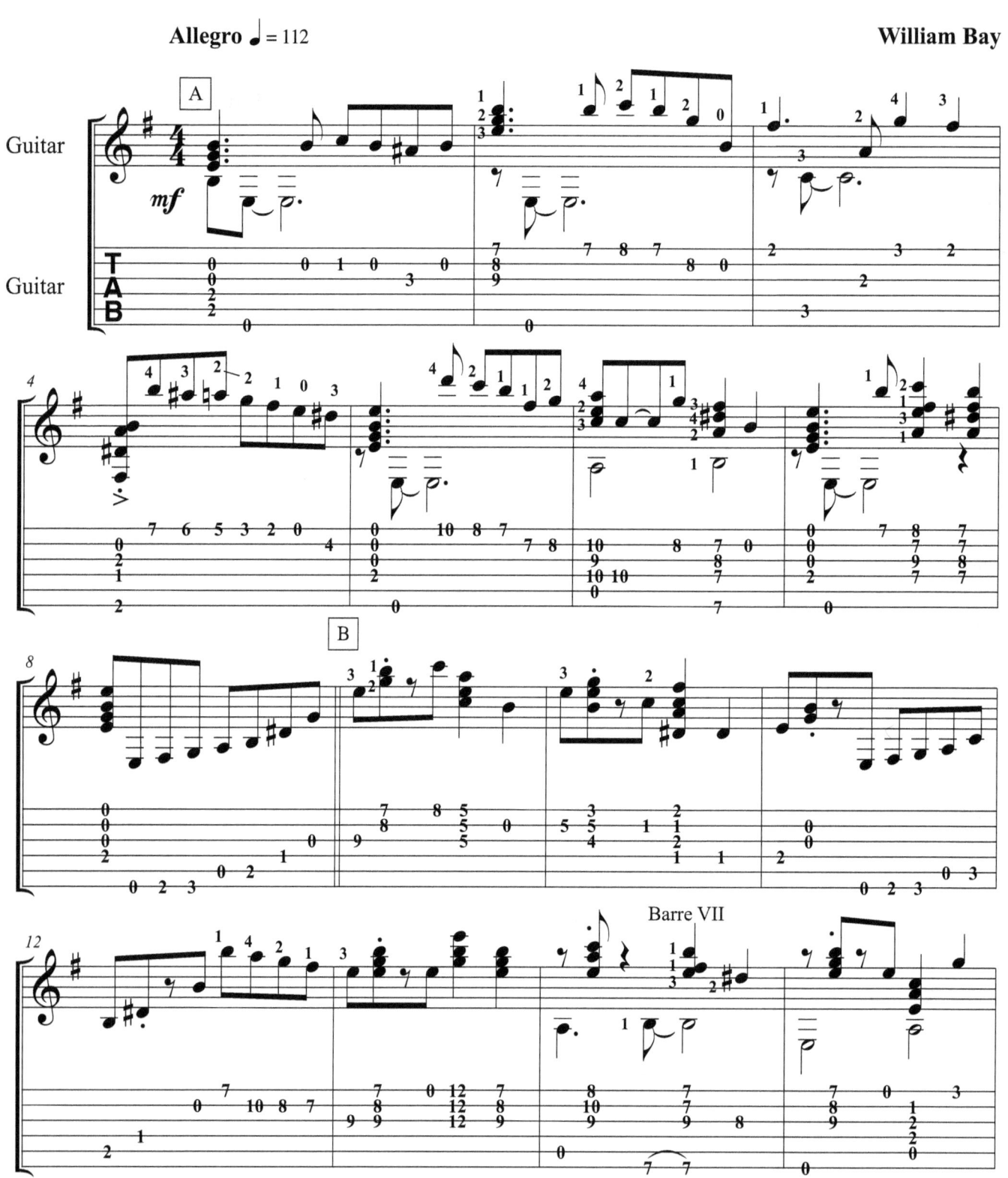

TANGO TWO

William Bay

TANGO FOUR

William Bay

Allegro ♩ = 122

© 2012 by William Bay. All Rights Reserved. BMI.

TANGO SEVEN

William Bay

TANGO EIGHT

William Bay

TANGO NINE

Dropped D Tuning

William Bay

Allegretto ♩ = 122

TANGO TEN

William Bay

TANGO ELEVEN

Dropped D Tuning

William Bay

TANGO TWELVE

William Bay

Allegro ♩ = 116

© 2012 by William Bay. All Rights Reserved. BMI.

TANGO THIRTEEN

William Bay

Slowly ♩ = 80

© 2012 by William Bay. All Rights Reserved. BMI.

Lucia

Dropped D Tuning

William Bay

www.ingramcontent.com/pod-product-compliance
Lightning Source LLC
LaVergne TN
LVHW061256060426
835507LV00020B/2337